DOT TO DOT
COUNTRYSIDE
SCENES
FOR ADULTS

This book includes 30 Unique Dot Pages.

Start from 1st Number dot and continue all the way till you reach end of numbers, all the designs are continous lines and there are no jumps or breaks!

If you have any suggestions or ideas, please drop an email to info@coloringbooks101.com

Copyright © 2021 by Sonia Rai

TABLE OF CONTENTS

Countryside Scene 1 (904 dots) - Black

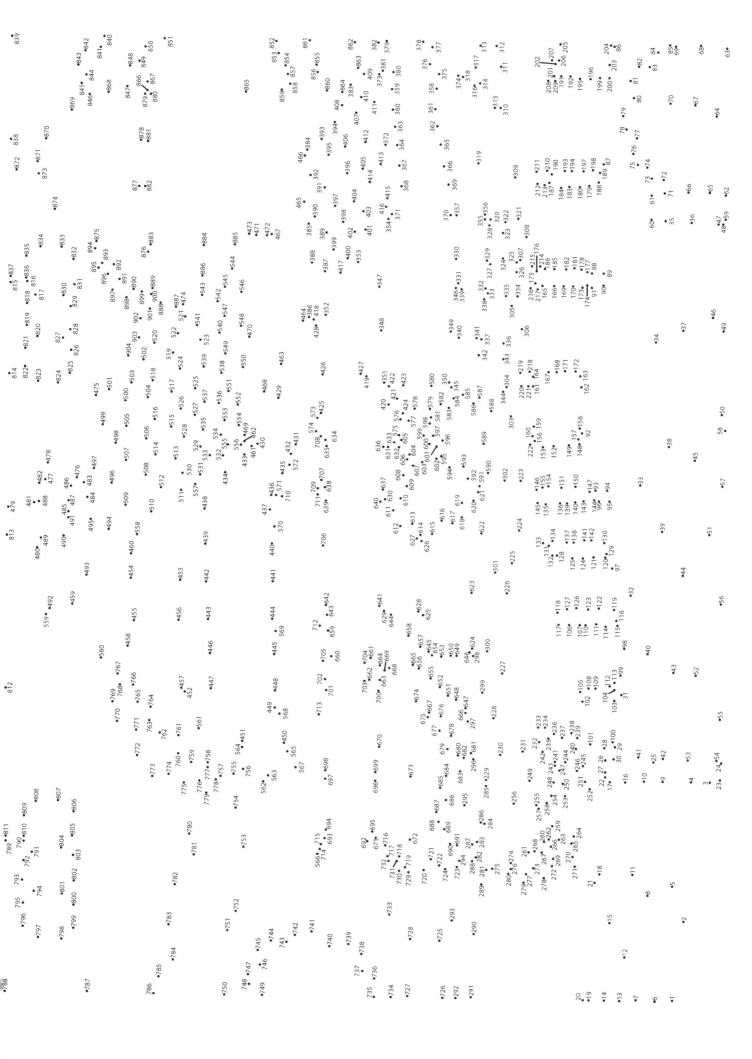

Countryside Scene 2 (925 dots) - Black

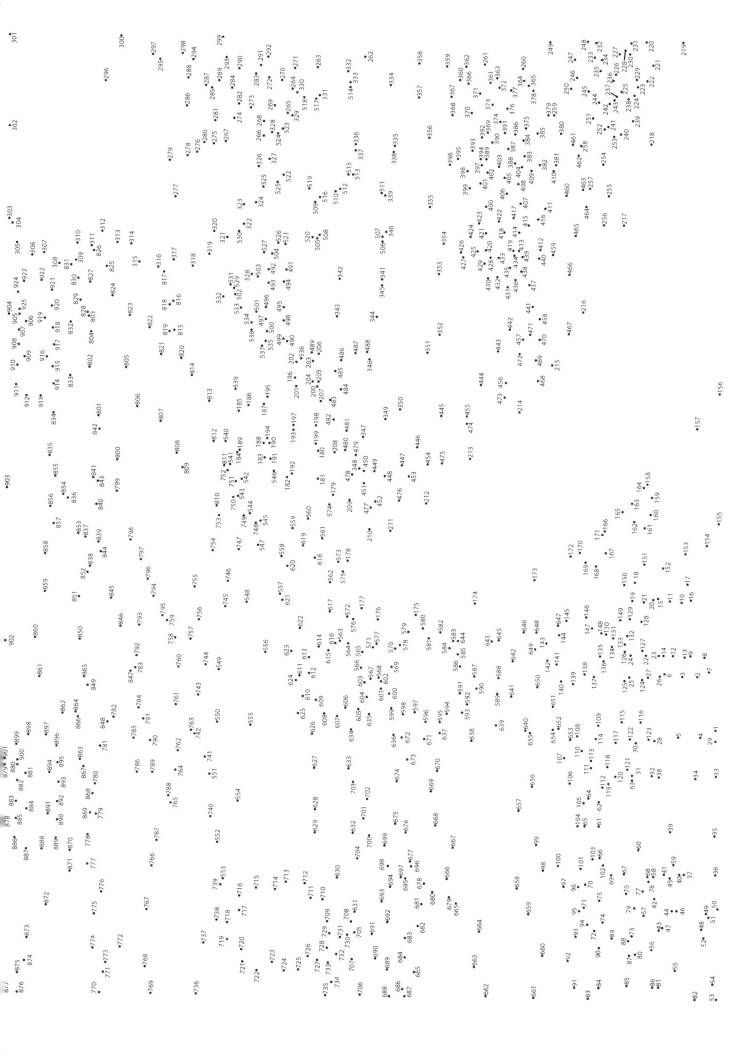

Countryside Scene 3 (827 dots) - Black

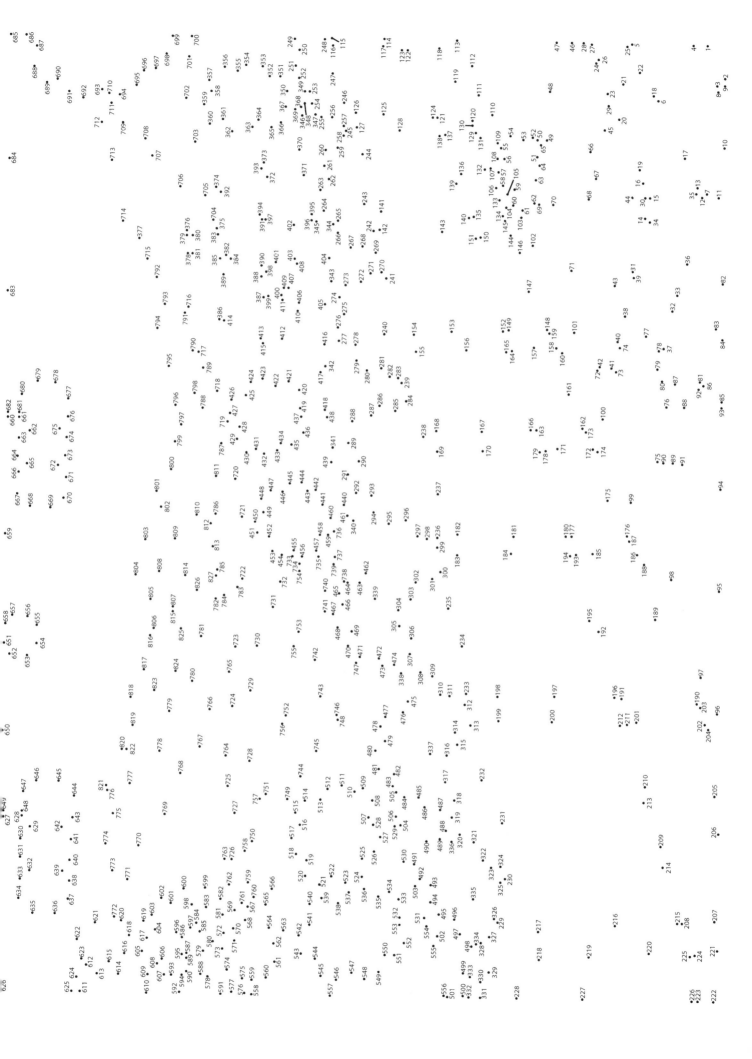

Countryside Scene 4 (768 dots) - Black

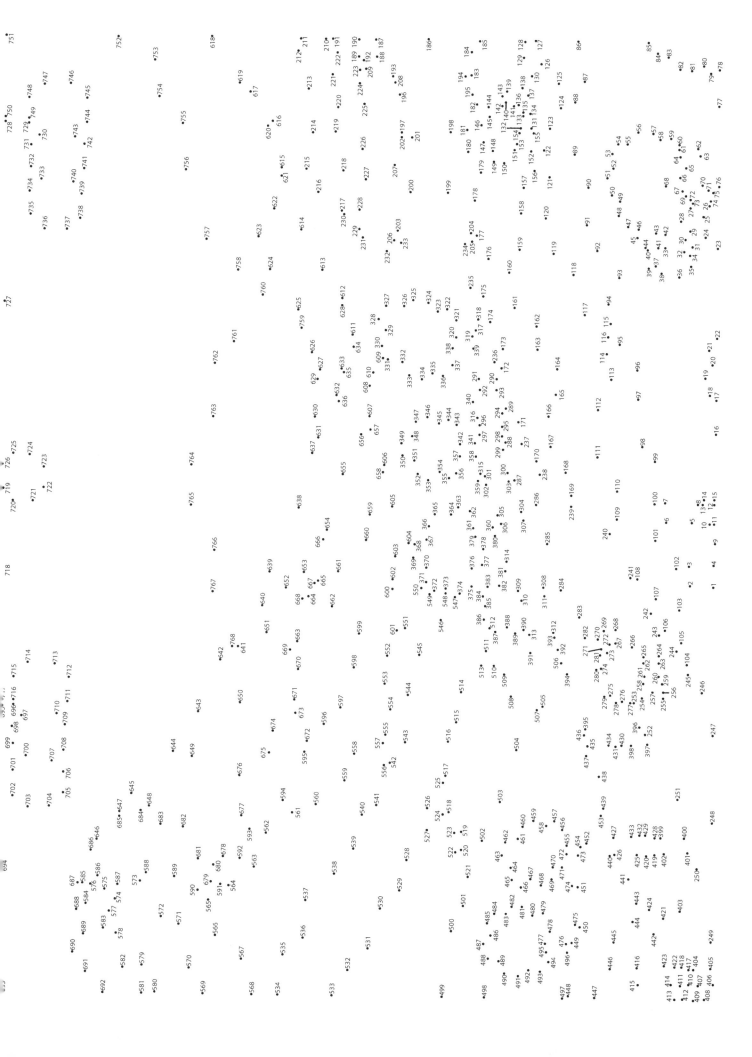

Countryside Scene 5 (751 dots) - Black

Countryside Scene 6 (789 dots) - Black

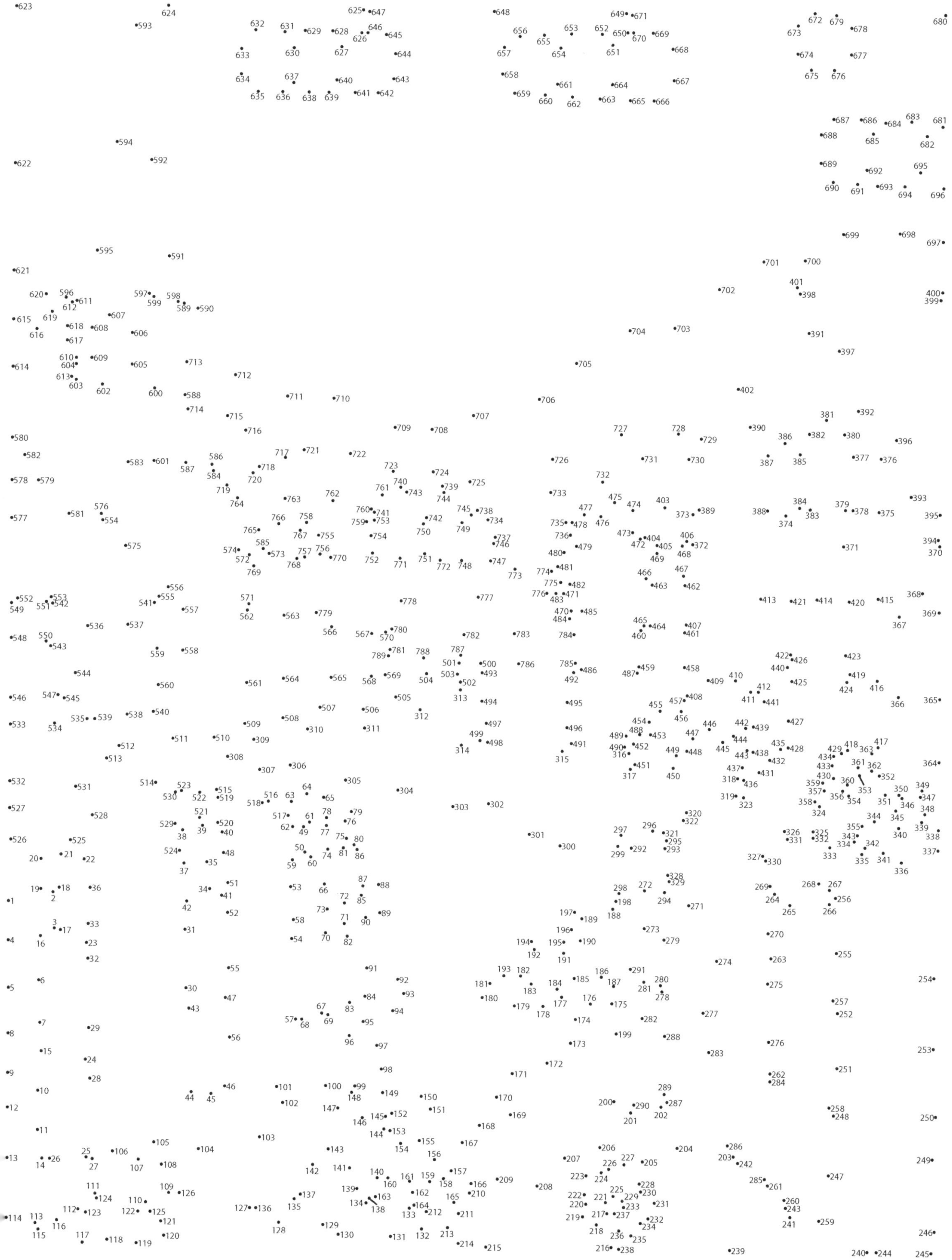

Countryside Scene 7 (899 dots) - Black

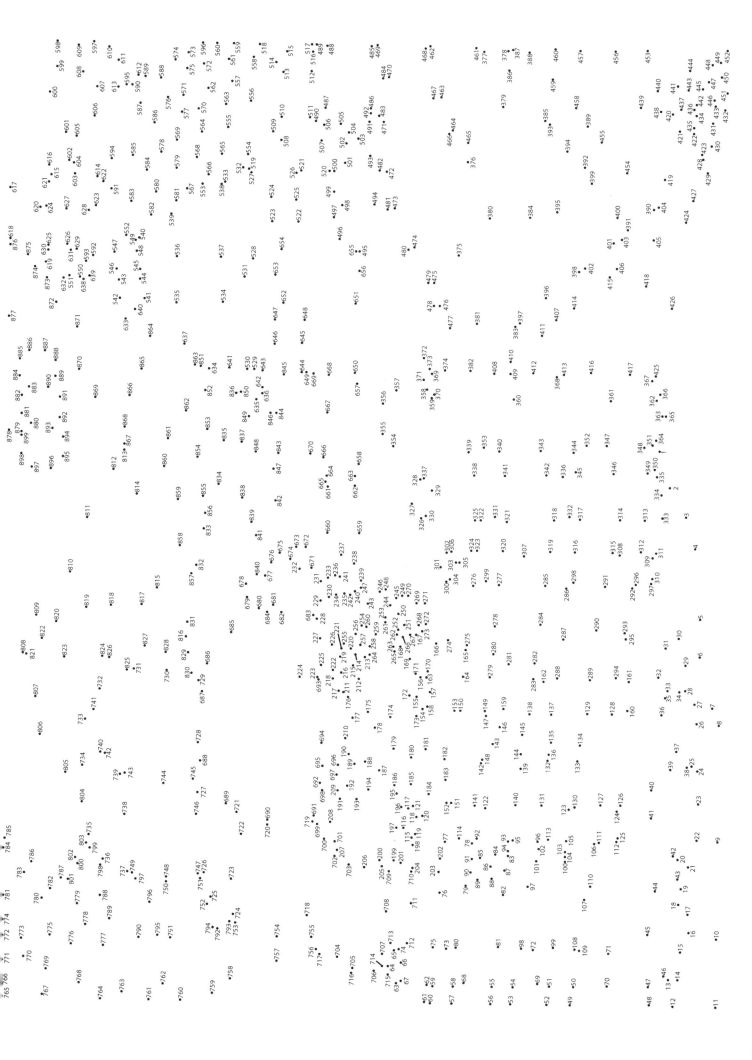

Countryside Scene 8 (611 dots) - Black

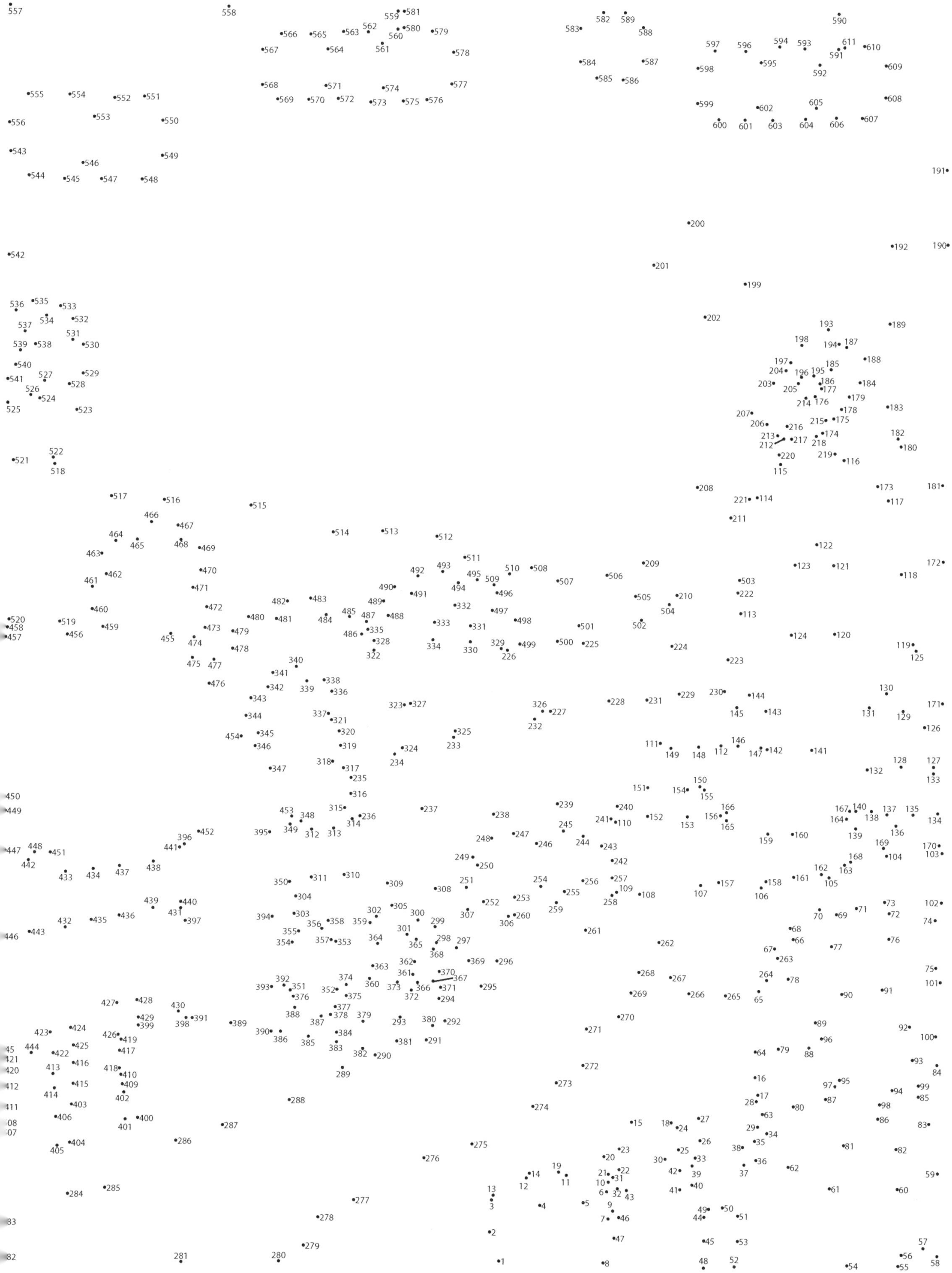

Countryside Scene 9 (698 dots) - Black

Countryside Scene 10 (764 dots) - Black

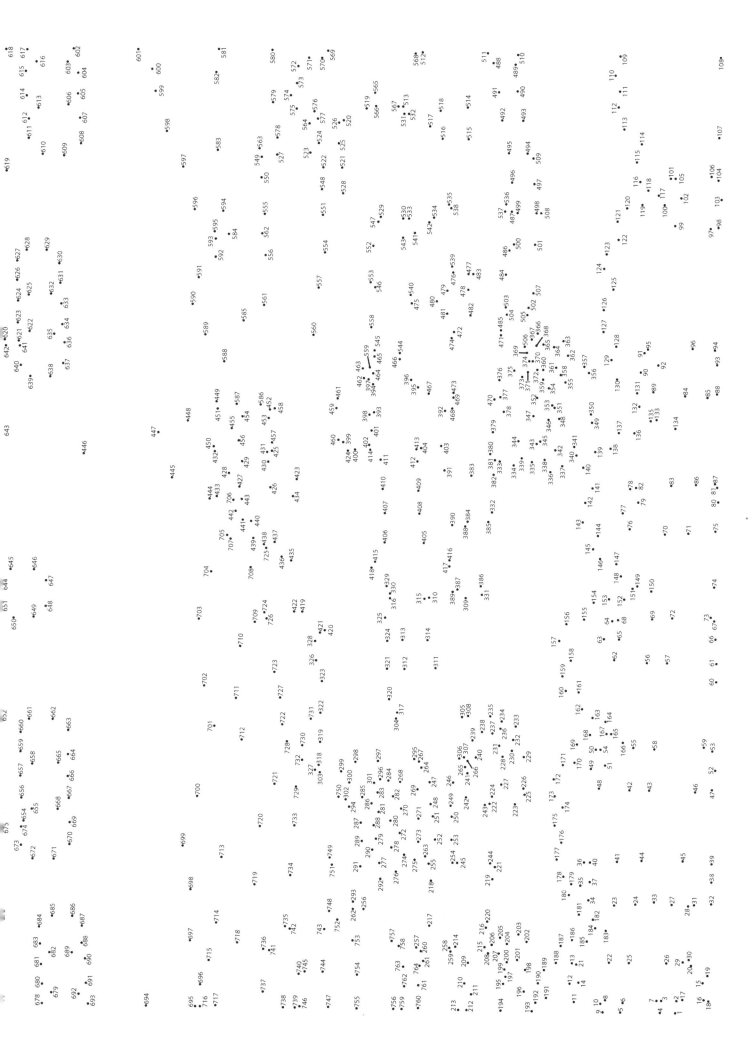

Countryside Scene 11 (762 dots) - Black

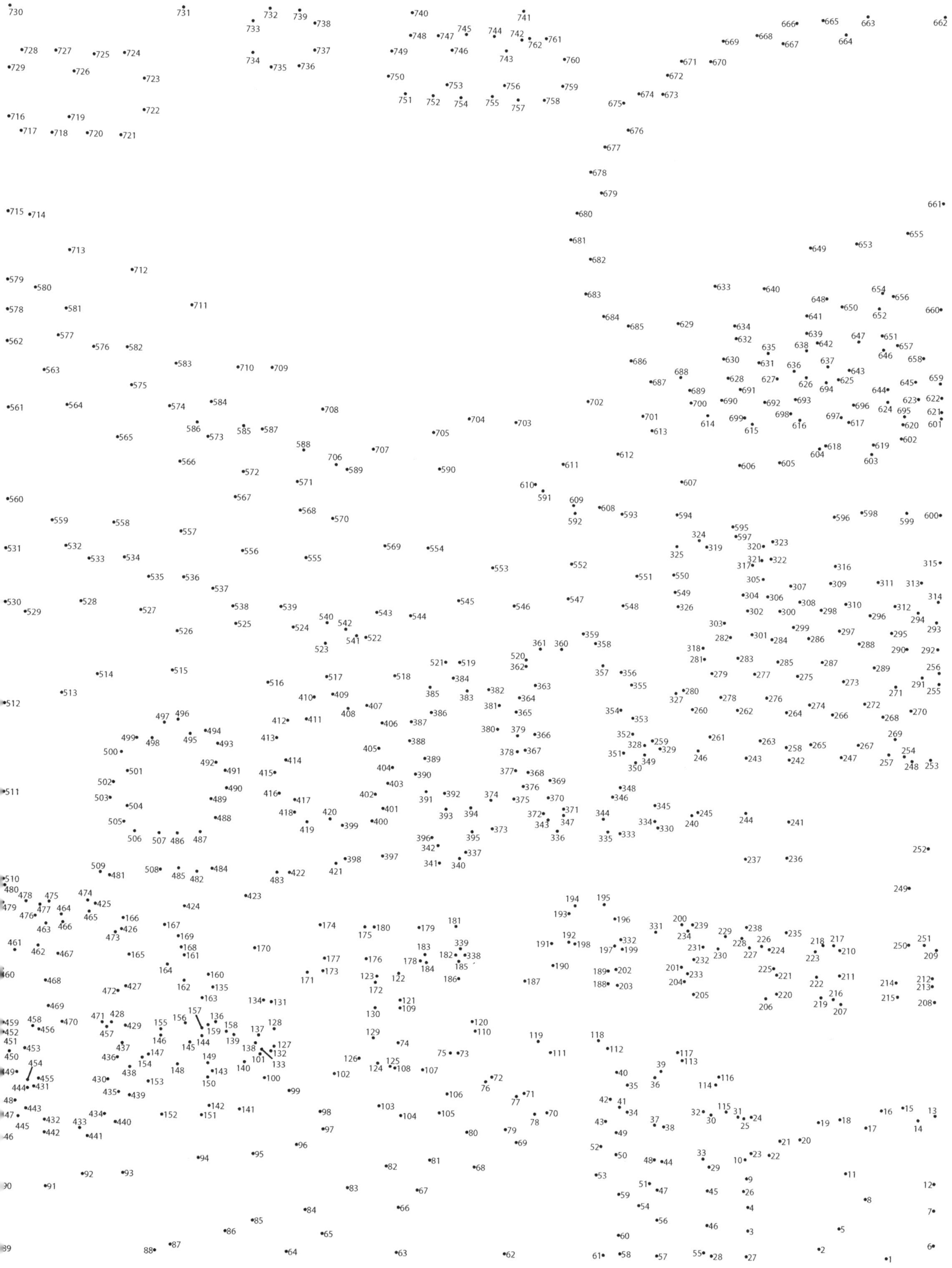

Countryside Scene 12 (809 dots) - Black

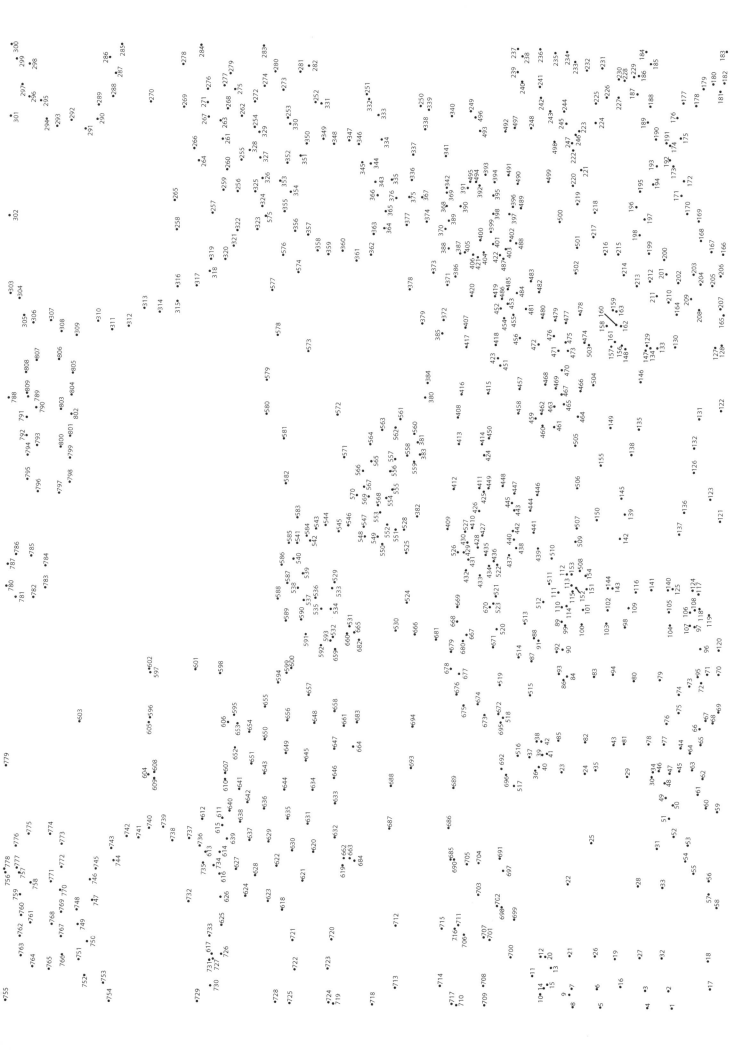

Countryside Scene 13 (655 dots) - Black

Countryside Scene 14 (728 dots) - Black

Countryside Scene 15 (841 dots) - Black

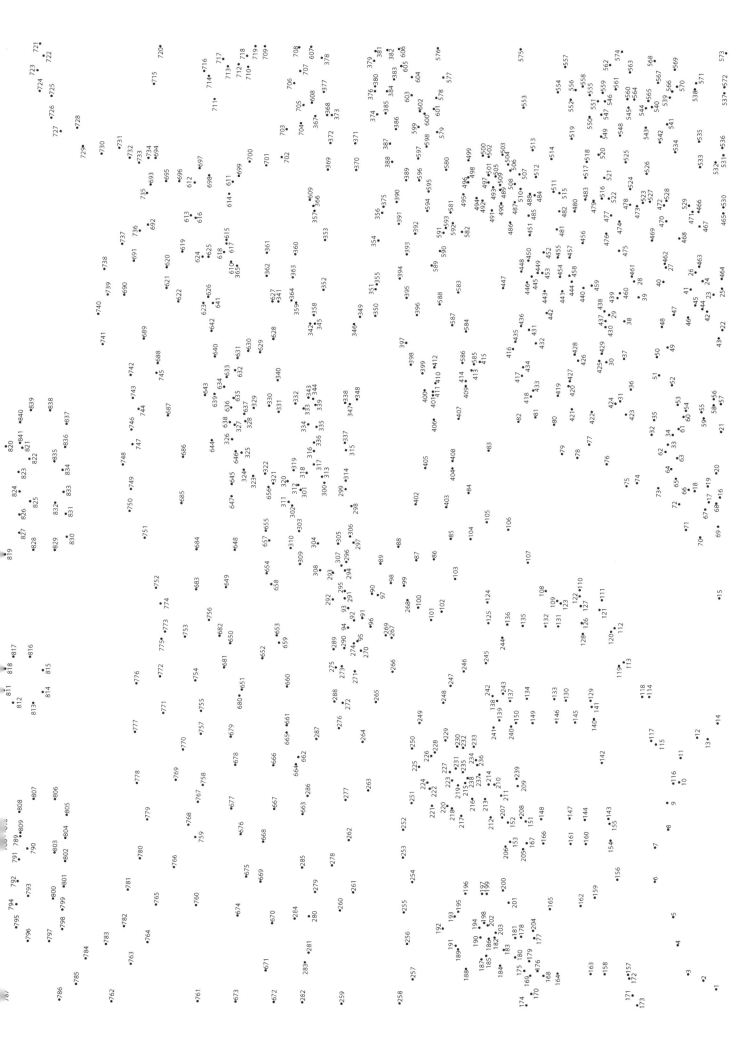

Countryside Scene 16 (839 dots) - Black

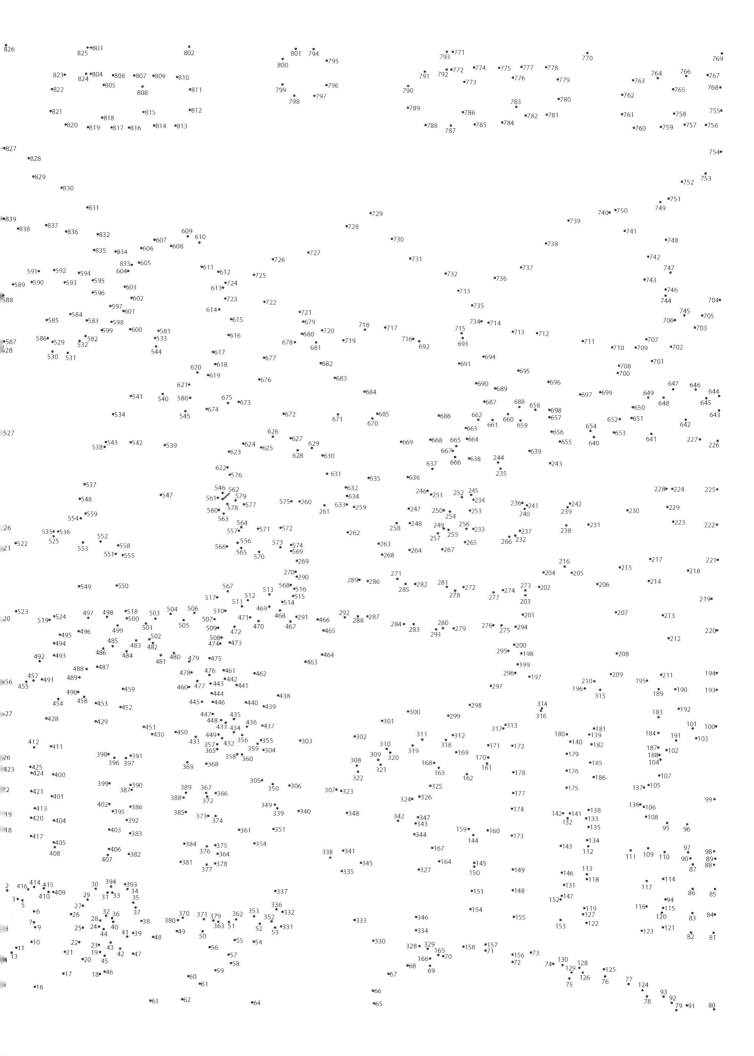

Countryside Scene 17 (773 dots) - Black

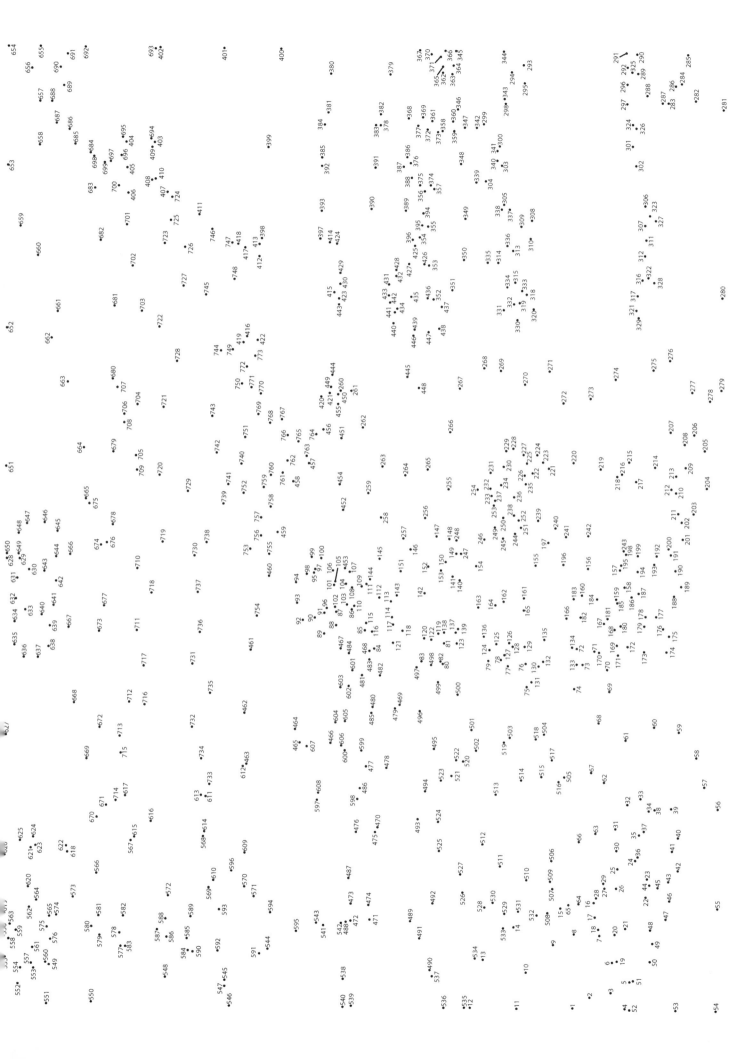

Countryside Scene 18 (780 dots) - Black

Countryside Scene 19 (751 dots) - Black

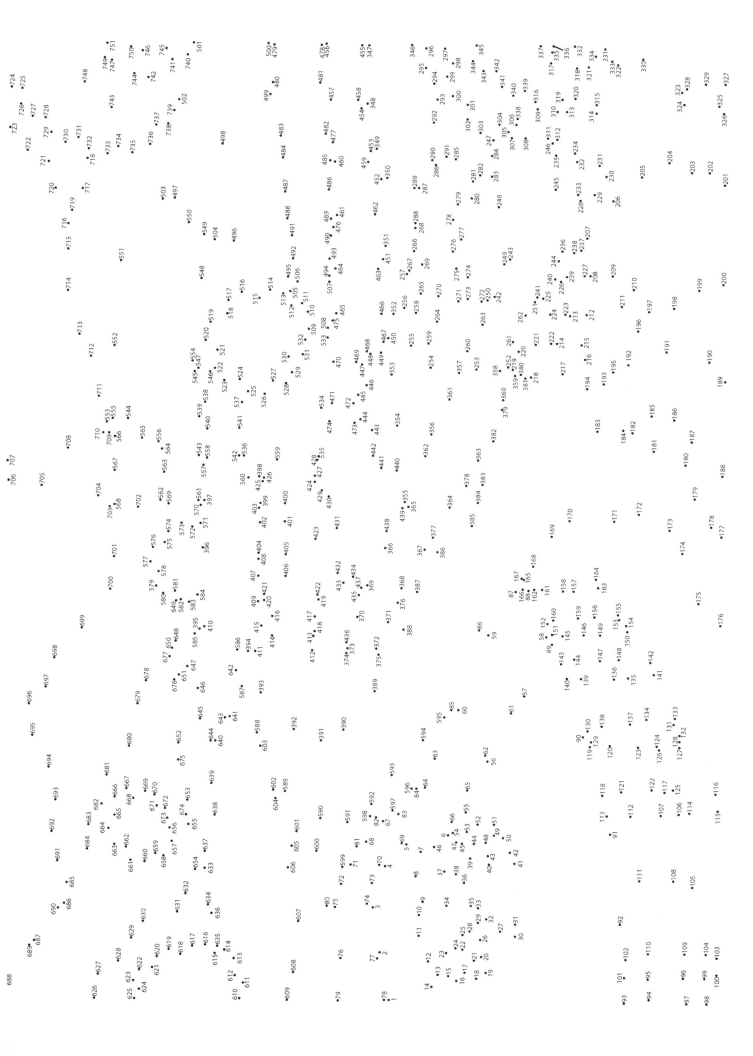

Countryside Scene 20 (817 dots) - Black

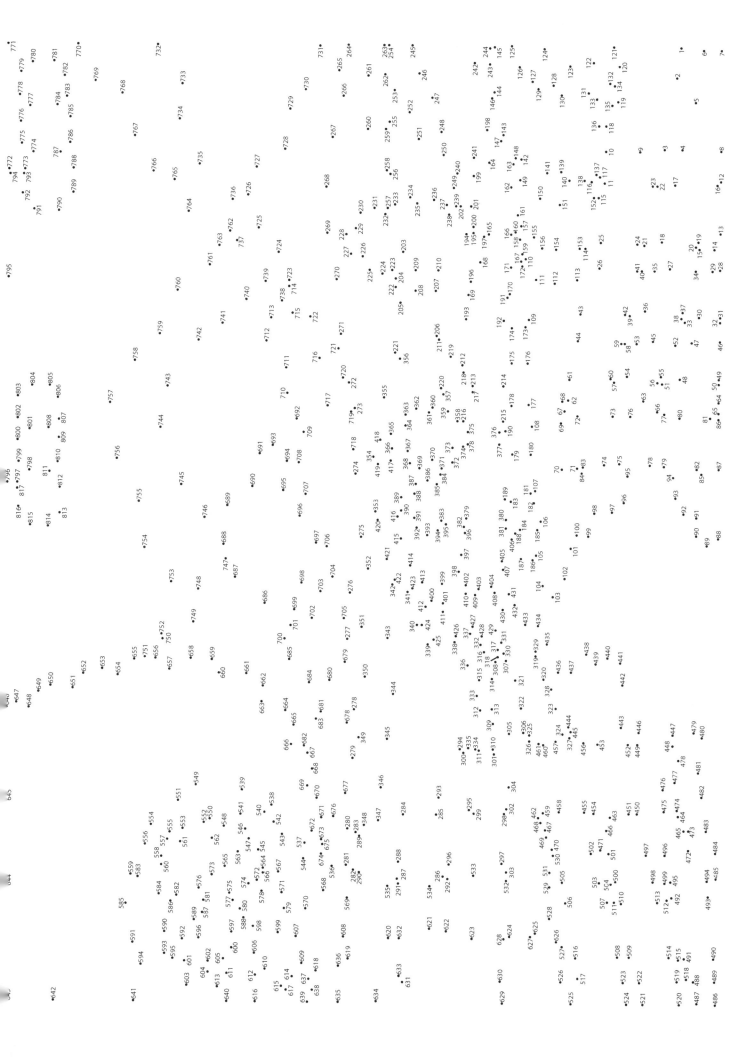

Countryside Scene 21 (727 dots) - Black

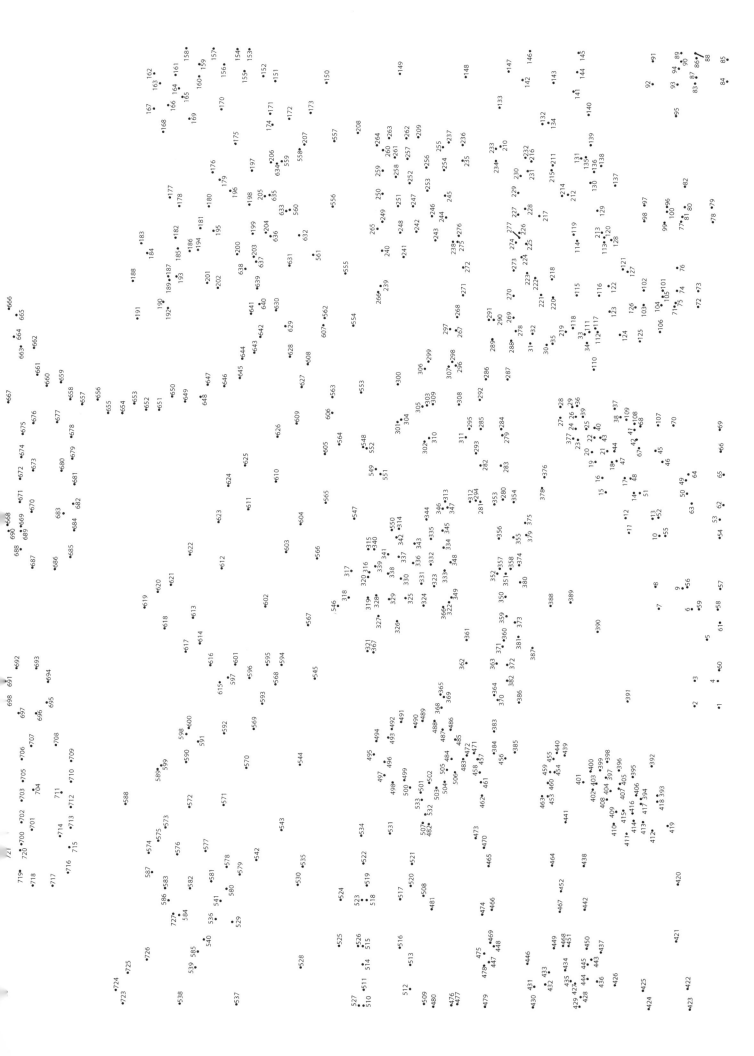

Countryside Scene 22 (757 dots) - Black

Countryside Scene 23 (870 dots) - Black

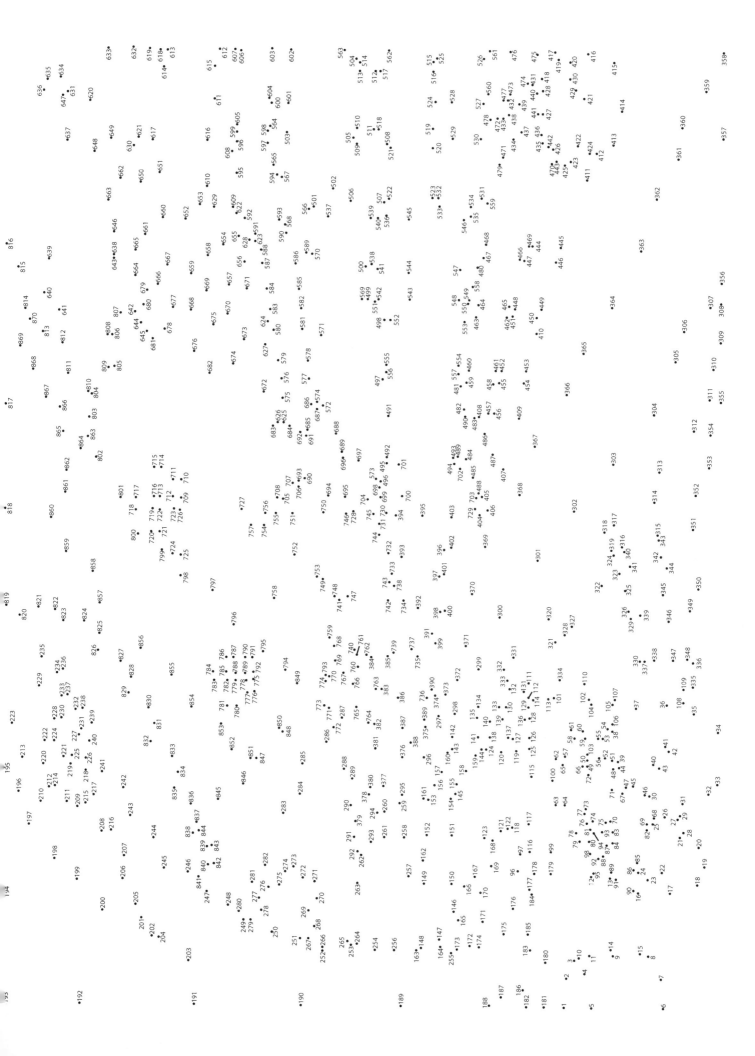

Countryside Scene 24 (825 dots) - Black

Countryside Scene 25 (717 dots) - Black

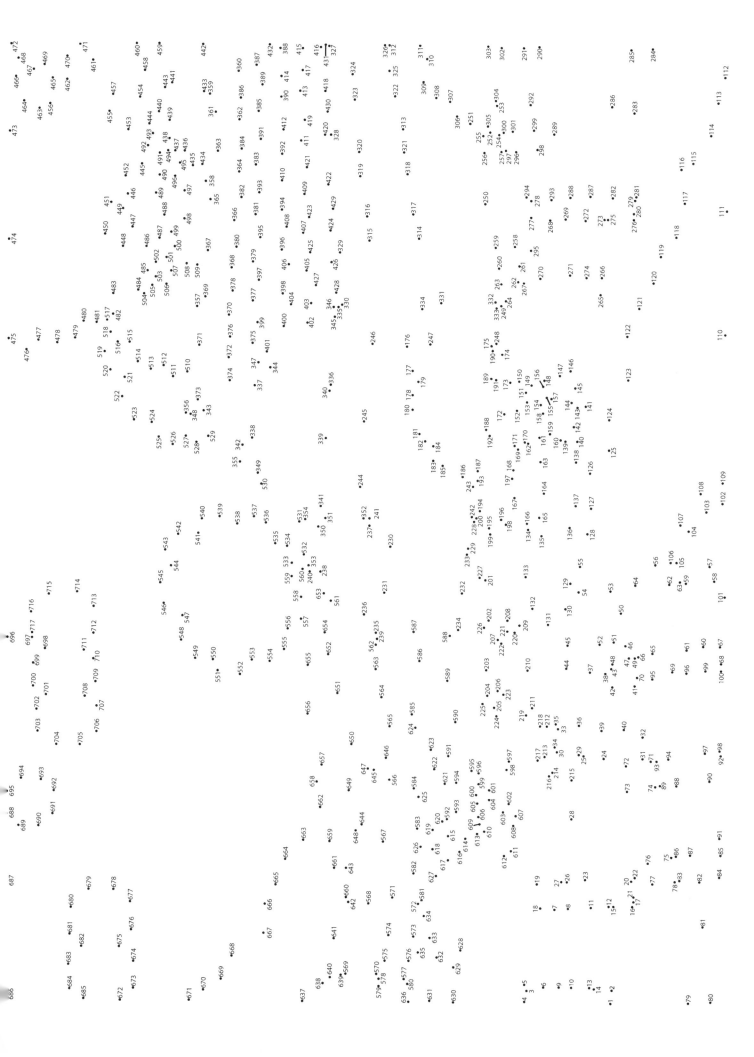

Countryside Scene 26 (809 dots) - Black

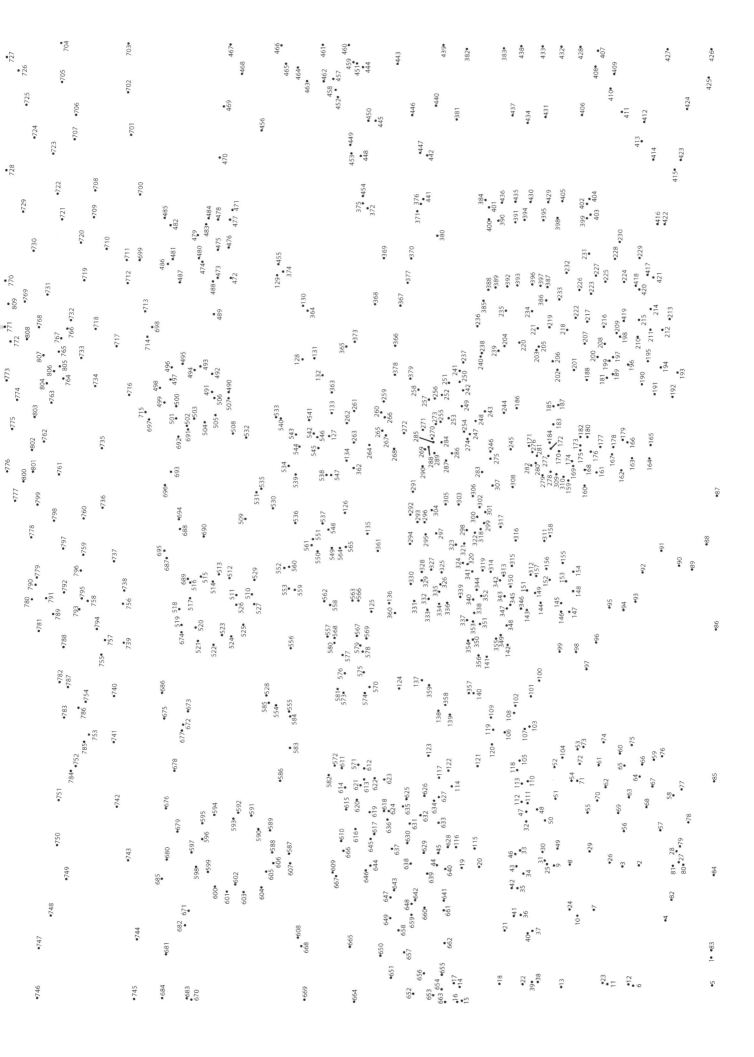

Countryside Scene 27 (814 dots) - Black

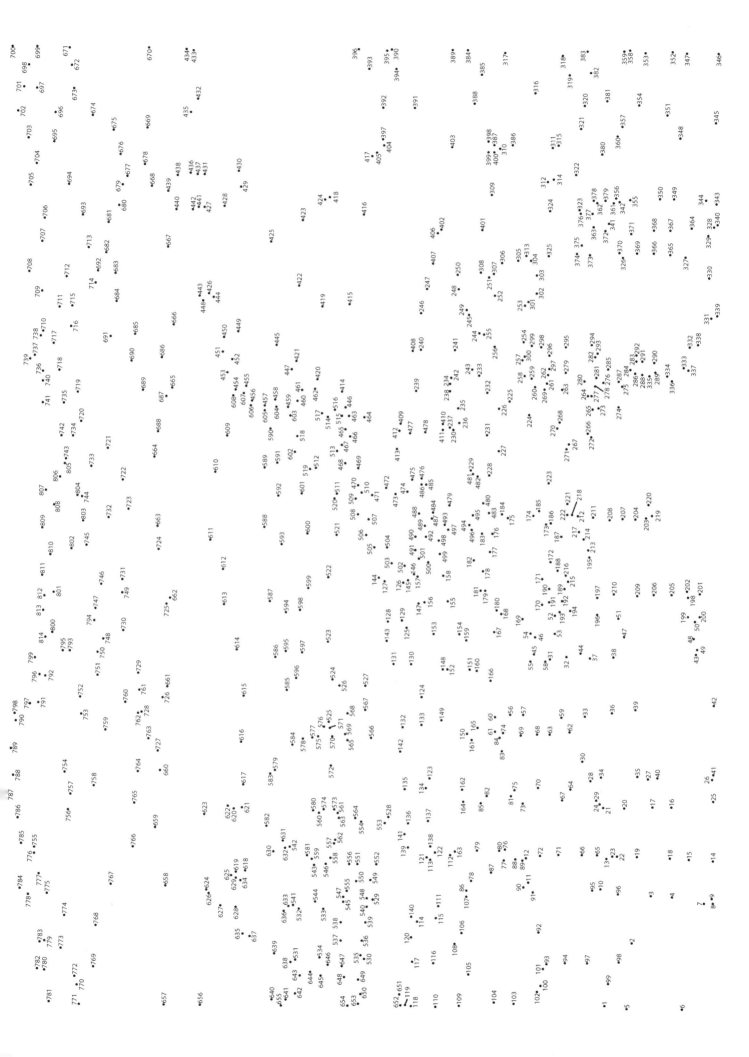

Countryside Scene 28 (653 dots) - Black

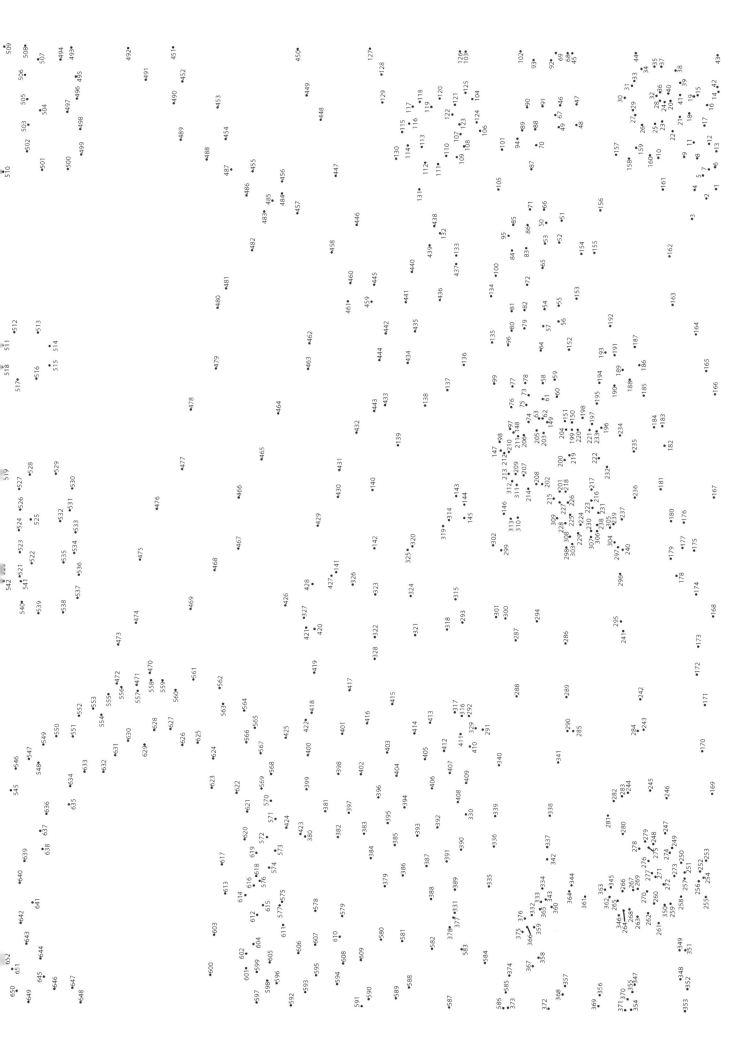

Countryside Scene 29 (912 dots) - Black

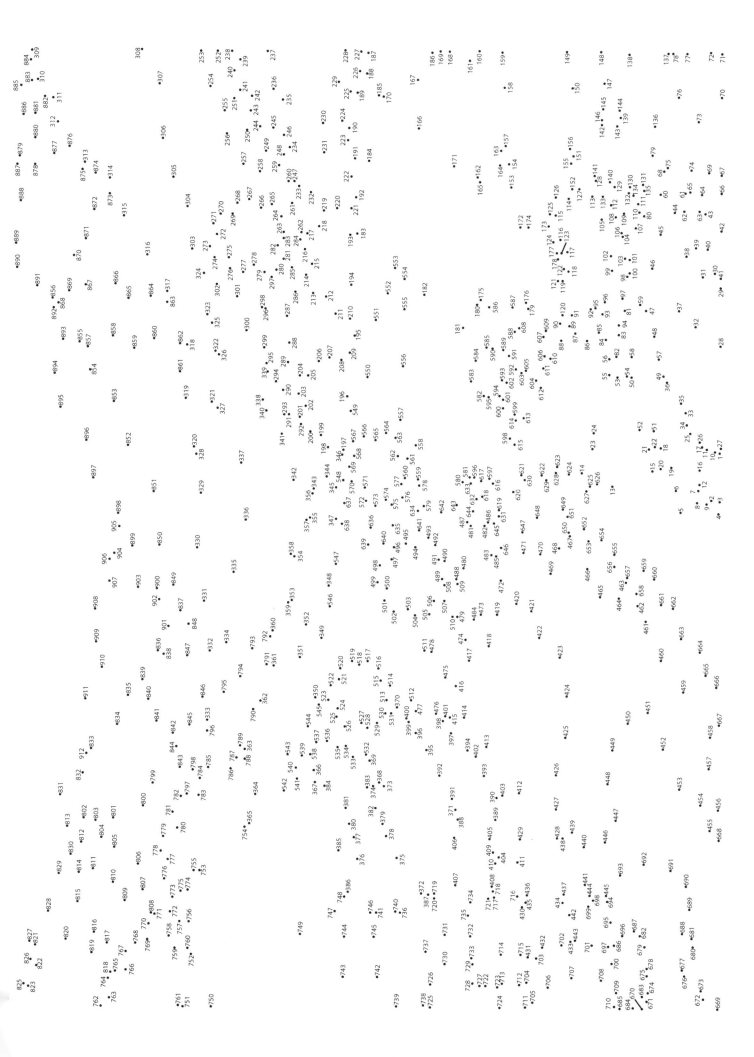

Countryside Scene 30 (729 dots) - Black

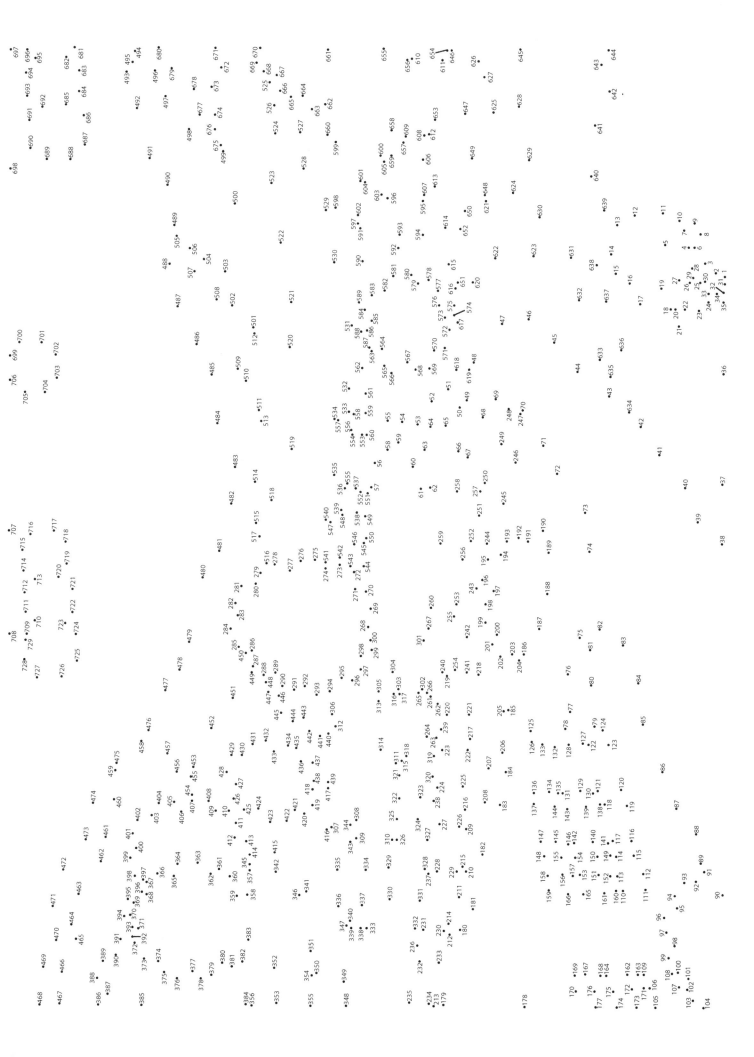

COMPELTED
DOT PAGES PREVIEWS

Completed Dot to Dot Pages Previews

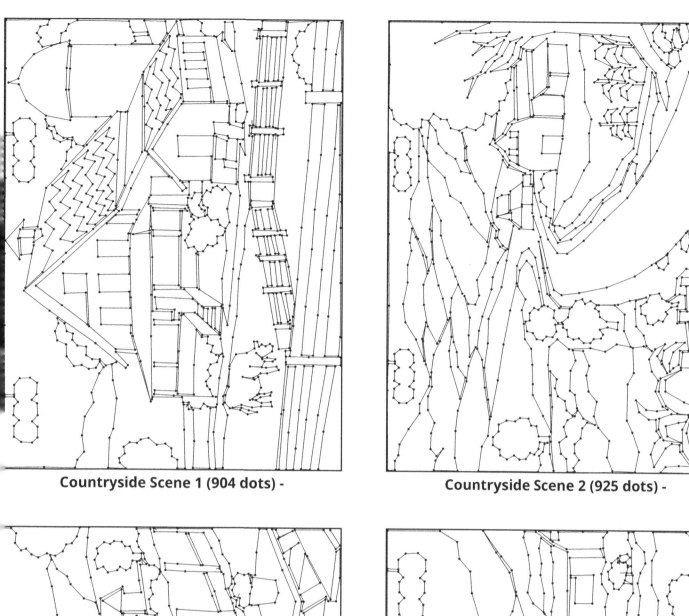

Countryside Scene 1 (904 dots) -

Countryside Scene 2 (925 dots) -

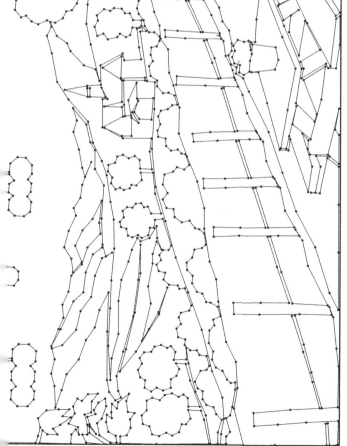

Countryside Scene 3 (827 dots) -

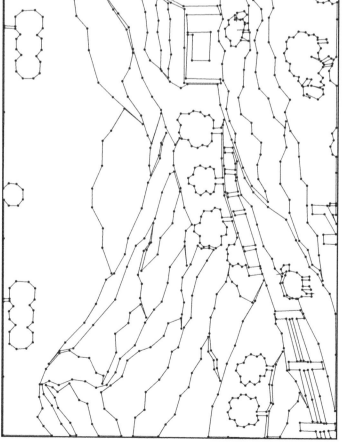

Countryside Scene 4 (768 dots) -

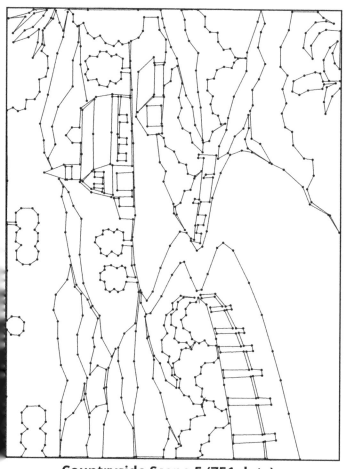

Countryside Scene 5 (751 dots) -

Countryside Scene 6 (789 dots) -

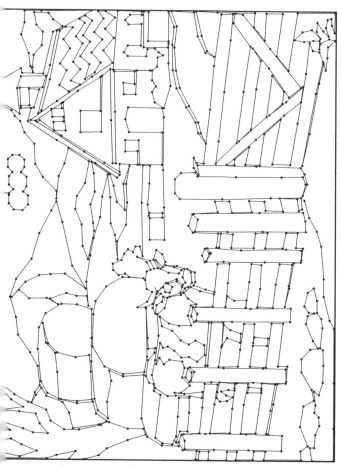

Countryside Scene 7 (899 dots) -

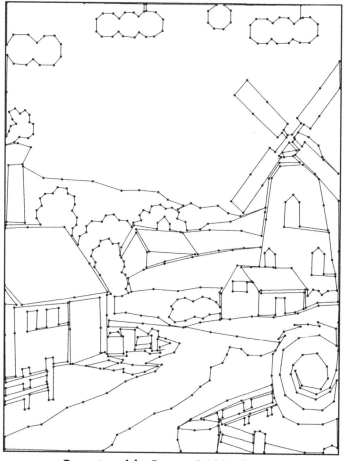

Countryside Scene 8 (611 dots) -

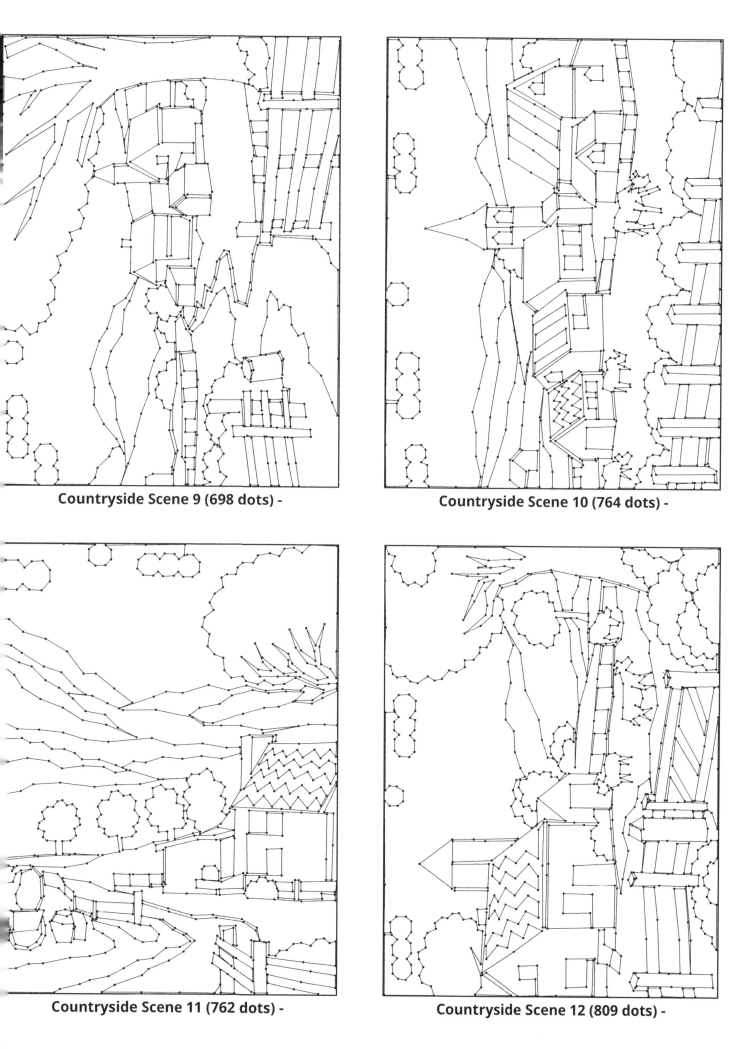

Countryside Scene 9 (698 dots) -

Countryside Scene 10 (764 dots) -

Countryside Scene 11 (762 dots) -

Countryside Scene 12 (809 dots) -

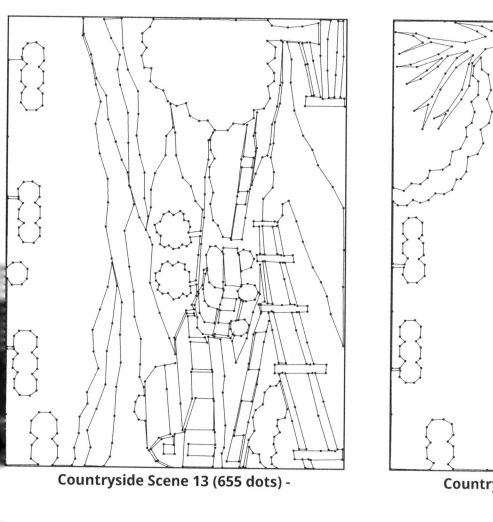

Countryside Scene 13 (655 dots) -

Countryside Scene 14 (728 dots) -

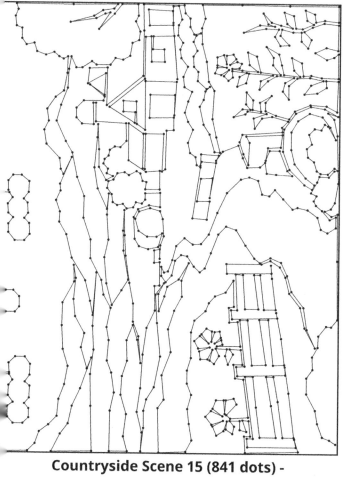

Countryside Scene 15 (841 dots) -

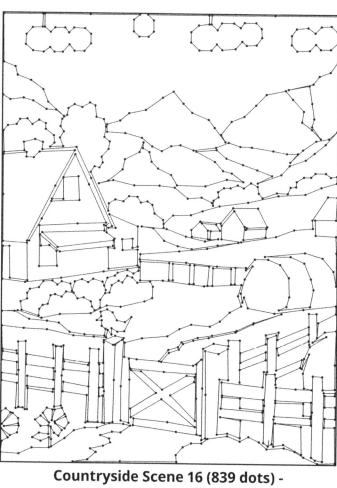

Countryside Scene 16 (839 dots) -

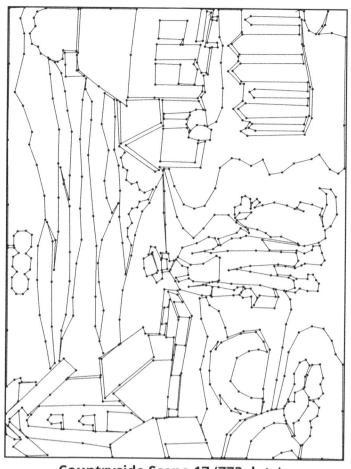

Countryside Scene 17 (773 dots) -

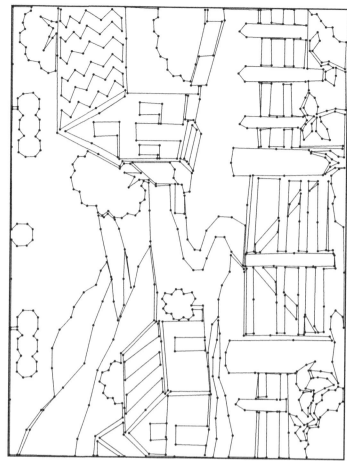

Countryside Scene 18 (780 dots) -

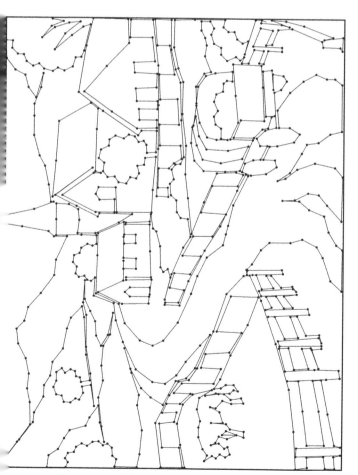

Countryside Scene 19 (751 dots) -

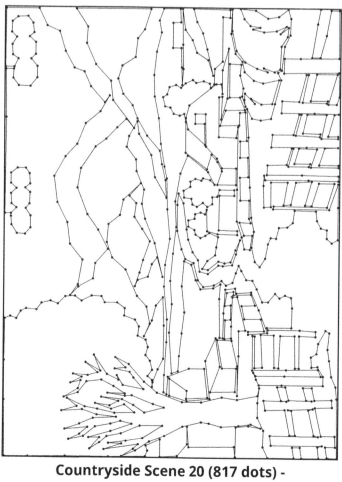

Countryside Scene 20 (817 dots) -

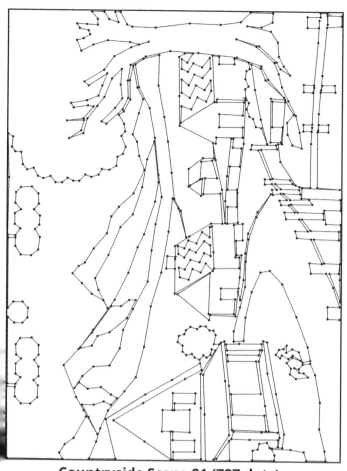

Countryside Scene 21 (727 dots) -

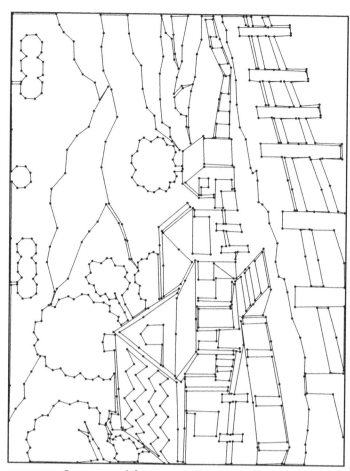

Countryside Scene 22 (757 dots) -

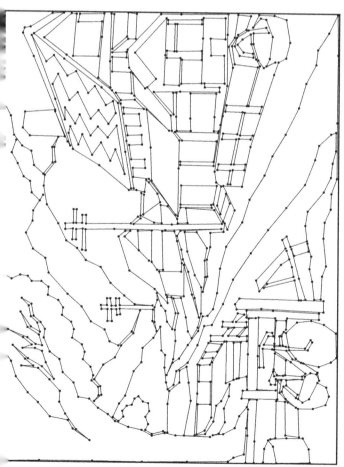

Countryside Scene 23 (870 dots) -

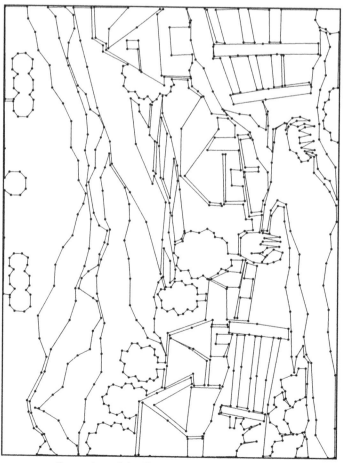

Countryside Scene 24 (825 dots) -

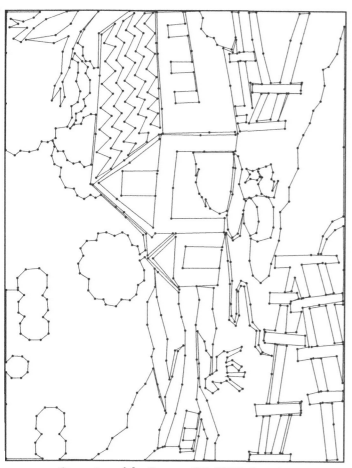

Countryside Scene 25 (717 dots) -

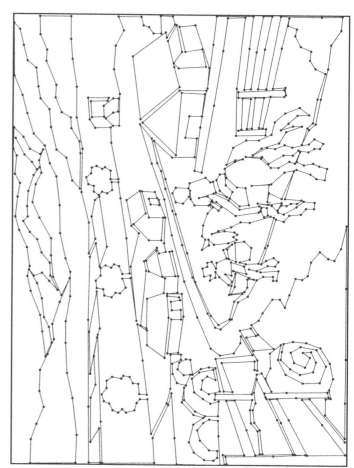

Countryside Scene 26 (809 dots) -

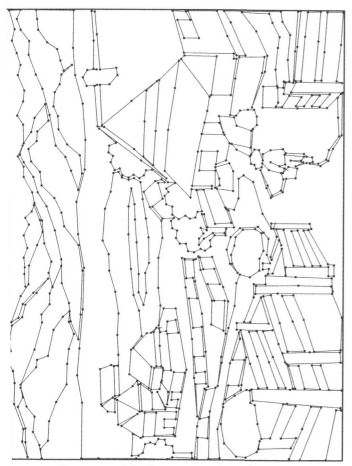

Countryside Scene 27 (814 dots) -

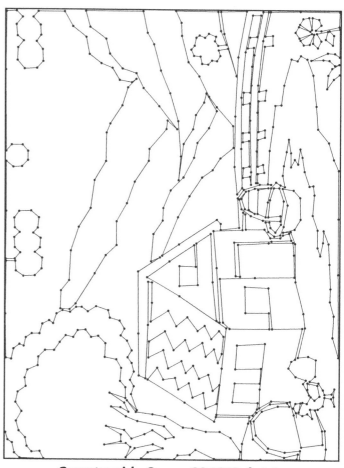

Countryside Scene 28 (653 dots) -

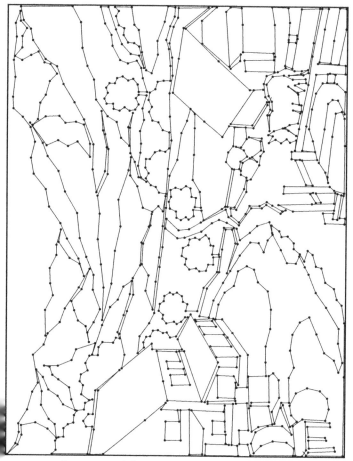

Countryside Scene 29 (912 dots) -

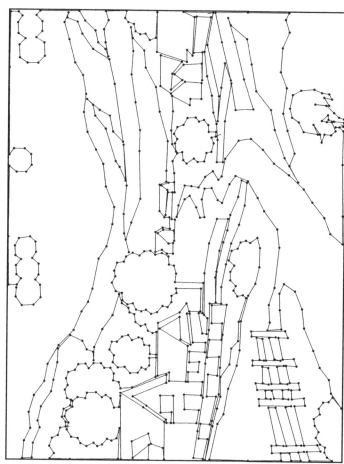

Countryside Scene 30 (729 dots) -